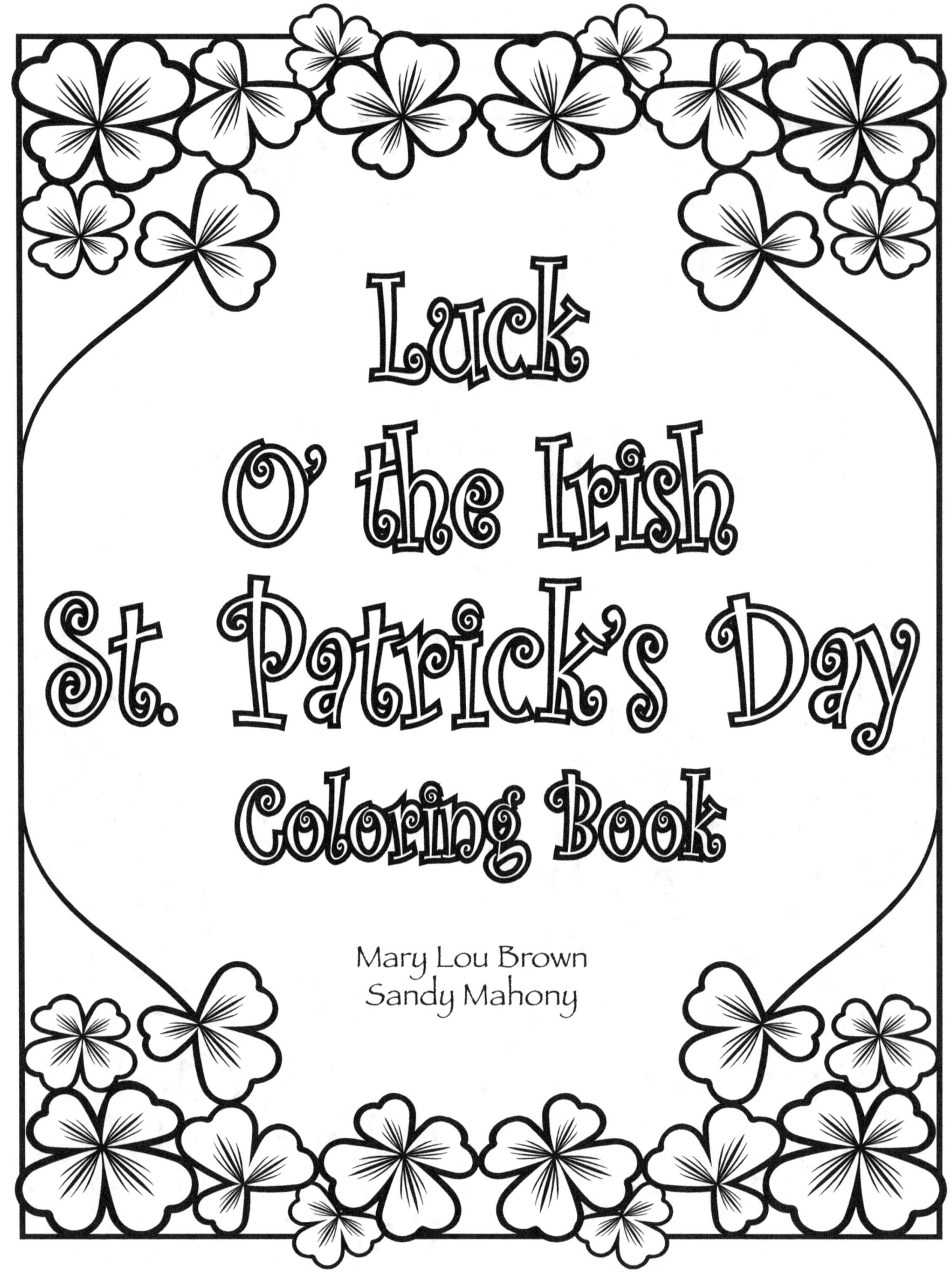

Luck O' the Irish St. Patrick's Day Coloring Book

Mary Lou Brown
Sandy Mahony

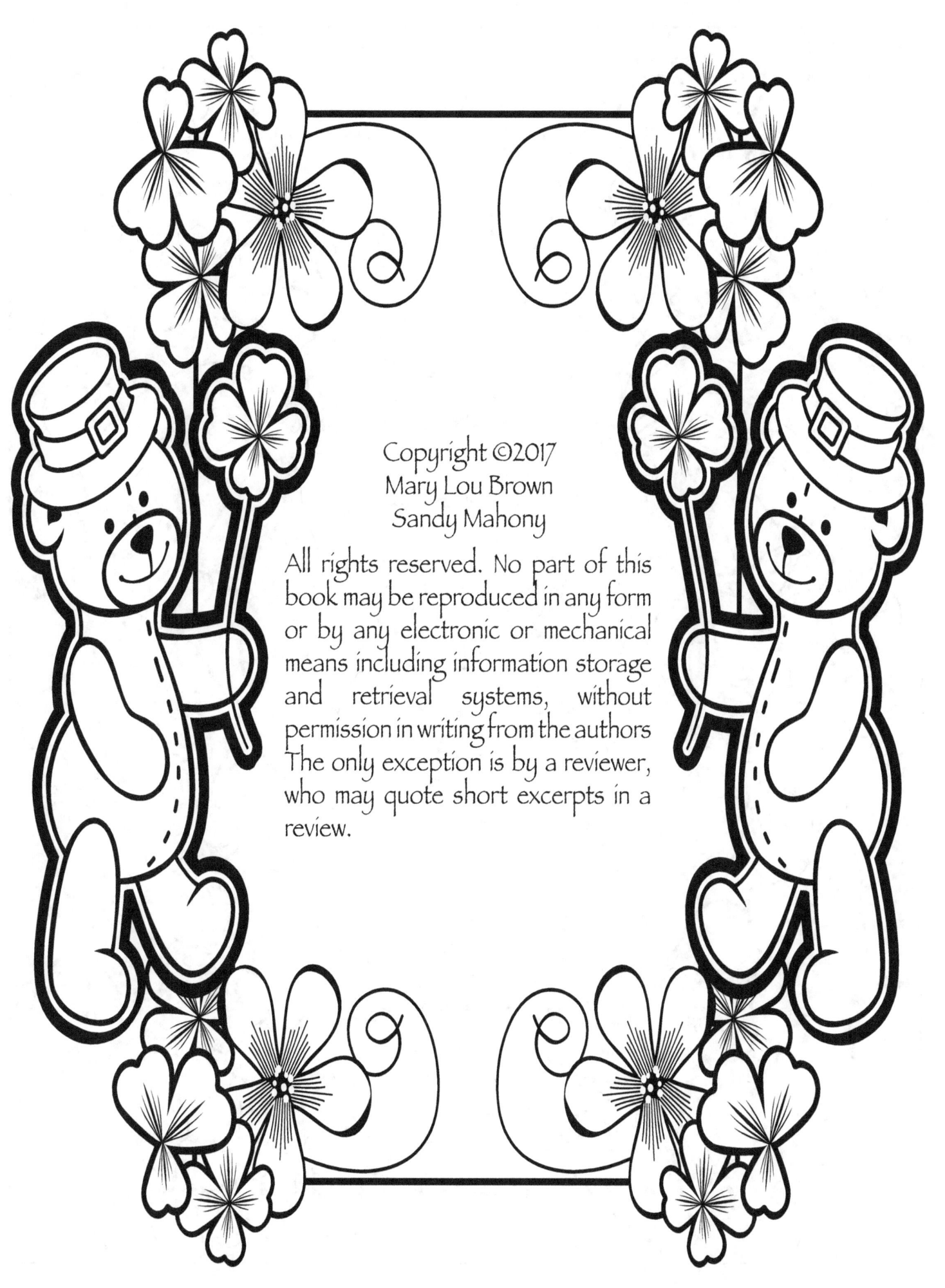

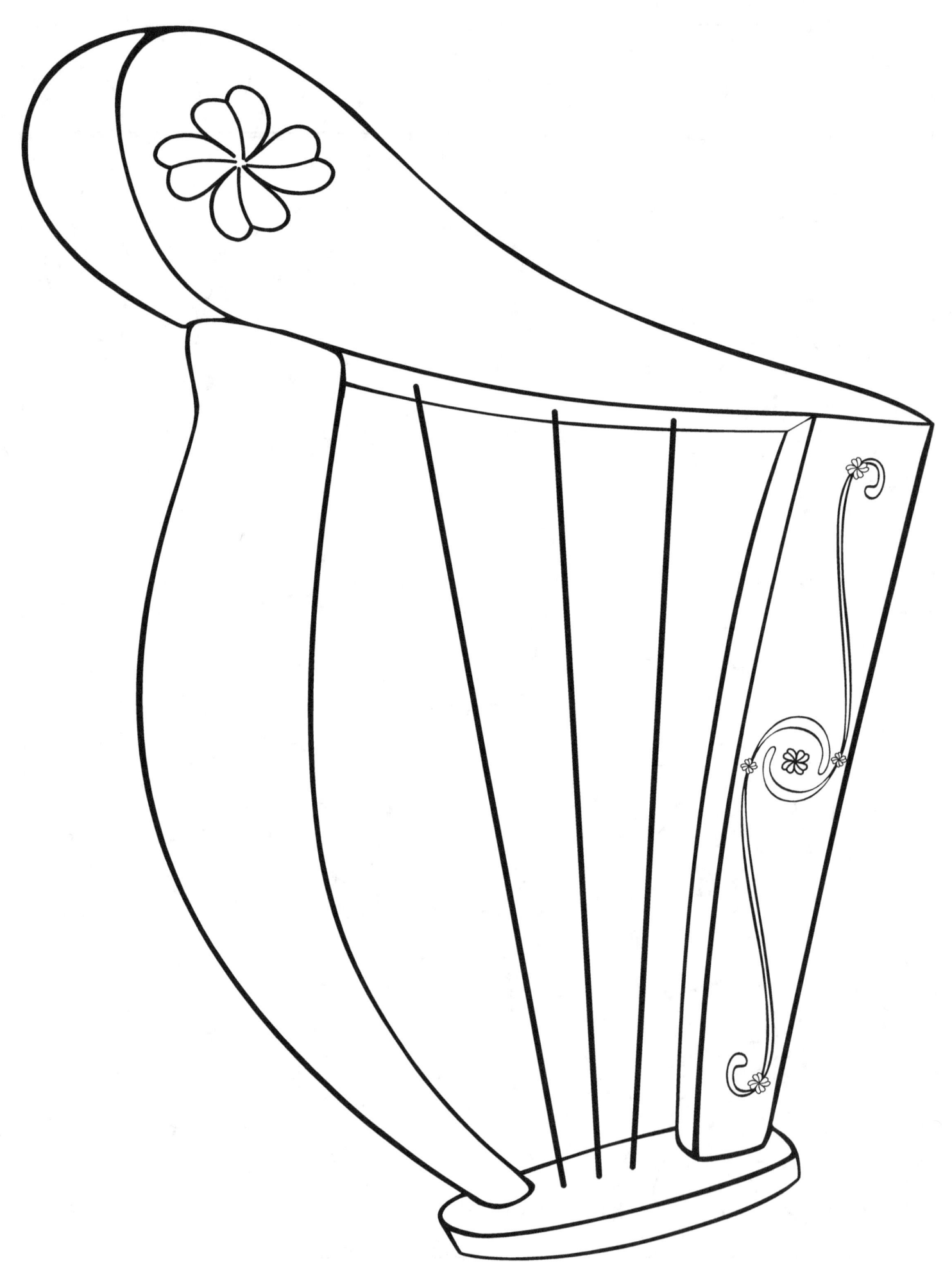

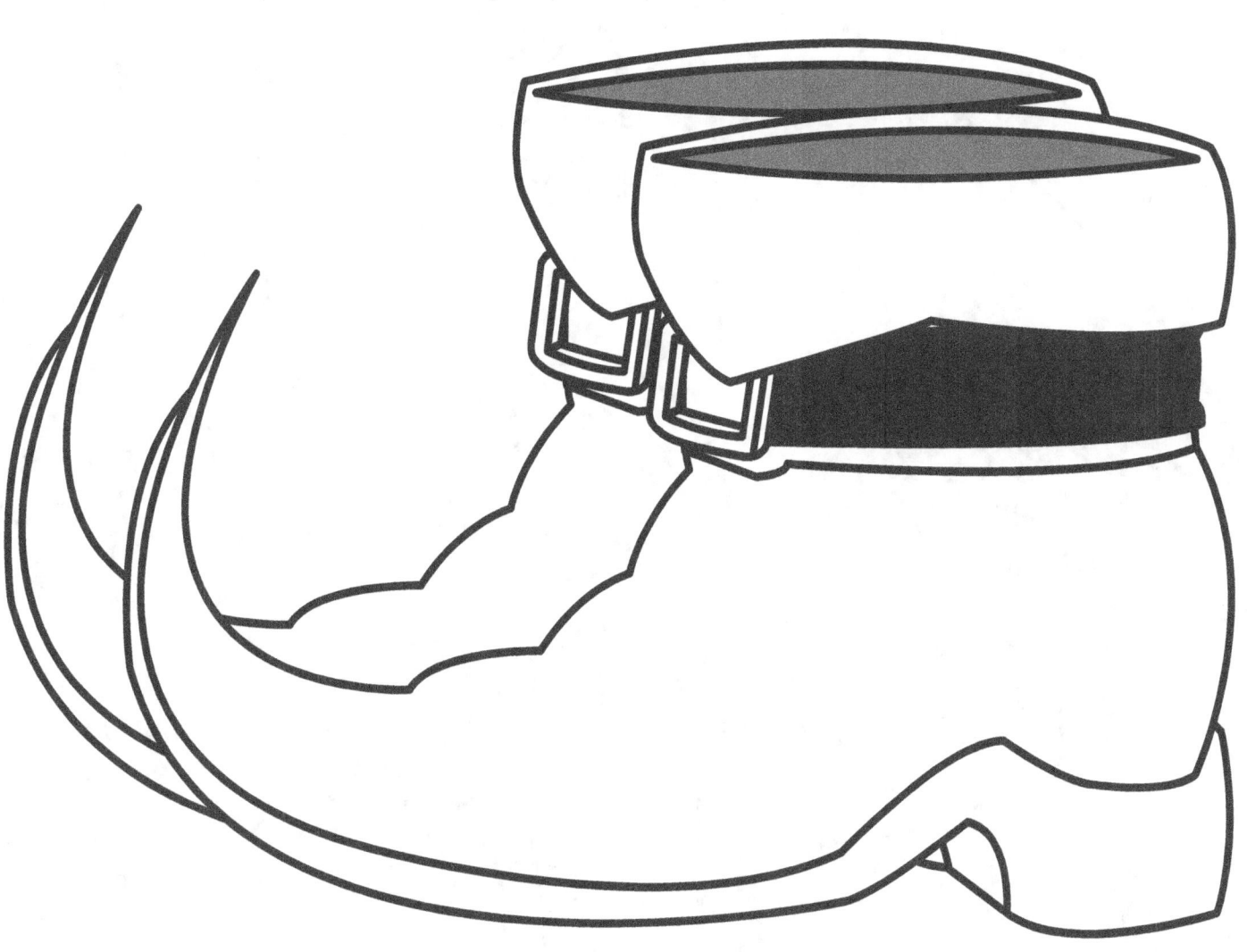

Leprechaun's House

Irish Castle

Color the Irish Flag from left to right:
green - white - orange

How many leprechauns do you see?

Who is lucky enough to find
the Blarney Stone?

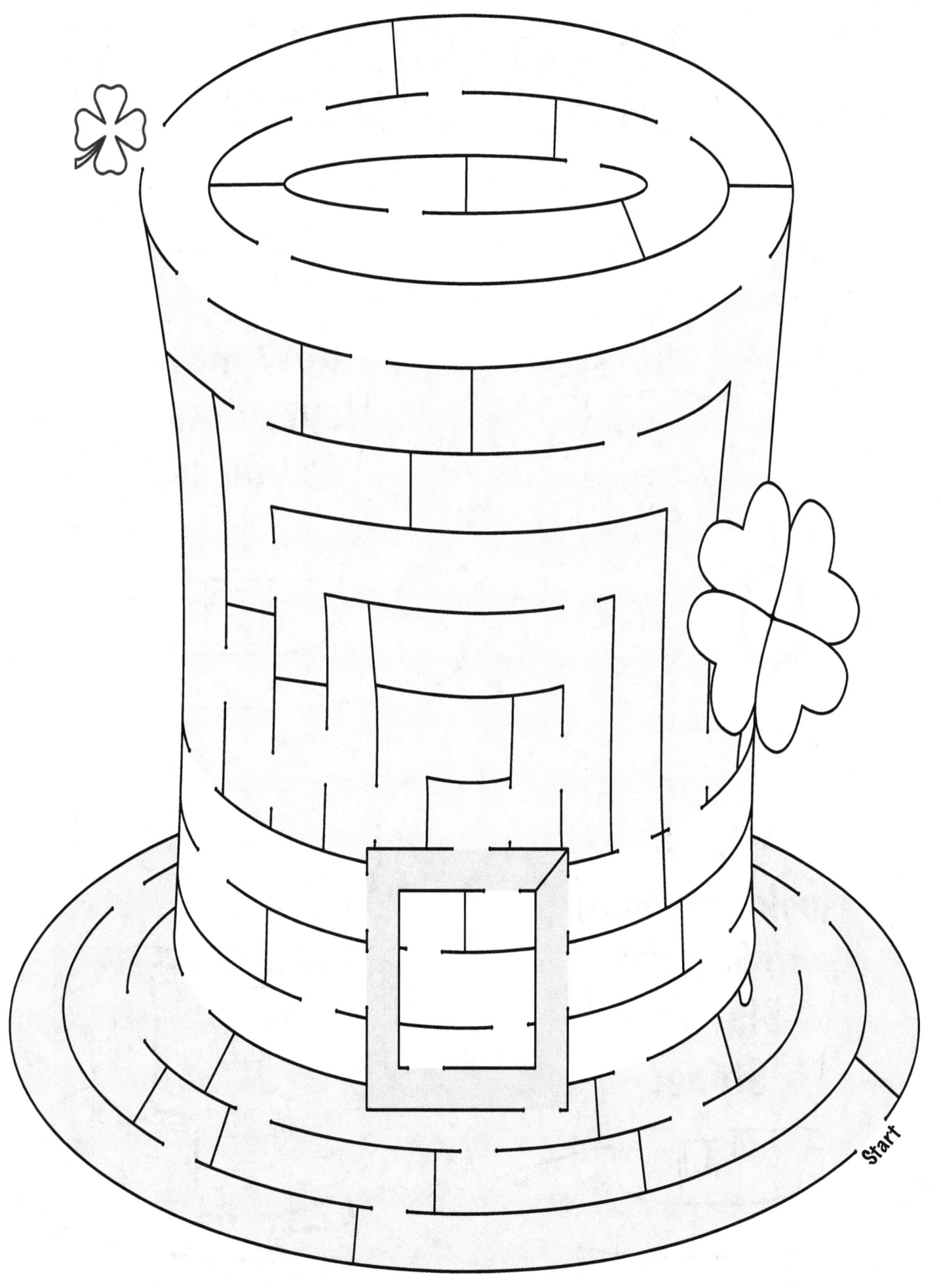

Start

ANSWERS

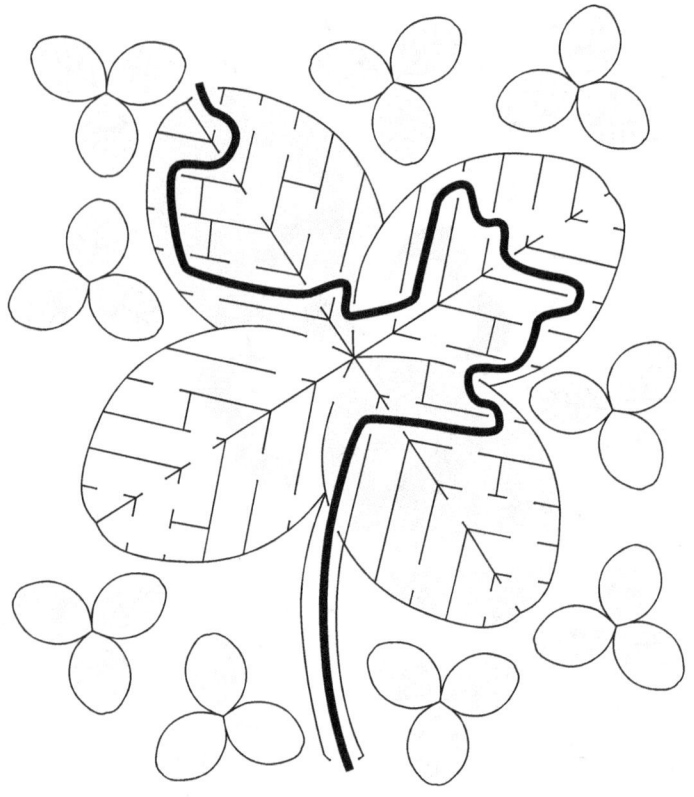

How many leprechauns do you see?

11

Who is lucky enough to find the Blarney Stone?

A

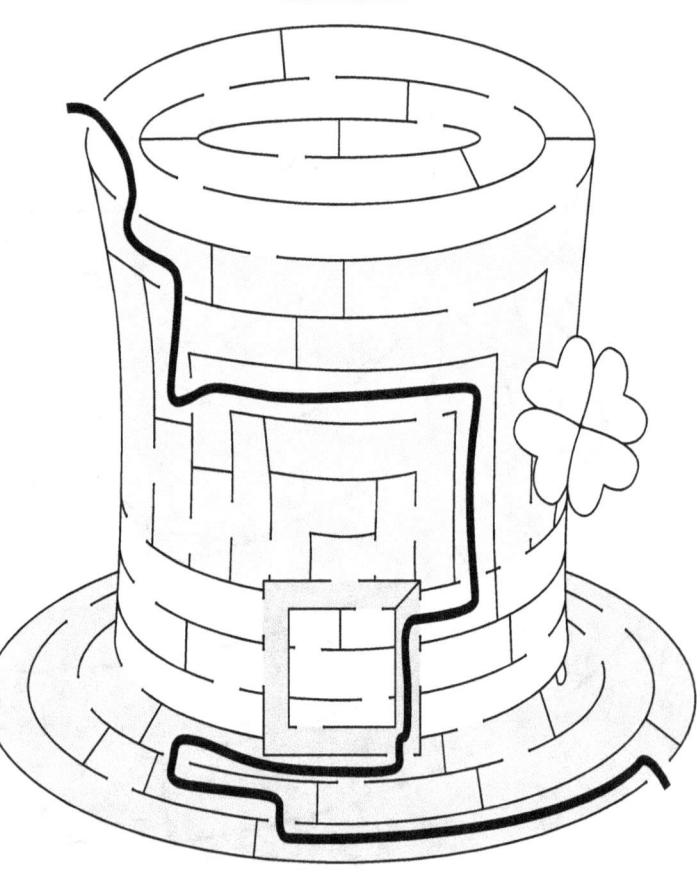

Good luck!